Searching for Sisterhood

A Memoir in Poems

Searching for Sisterhood

A Memoir in Poems

by

Christine Baldino O'Hanlon

Cover design by Shay Culligan
Cover image by Erv Dea-Jue
Author photo by Brian O'Hanlon

ISBN: 978-1-63980-850-2
Library of Congress Control Number: 2026931555

Kelsay Books
502 South 1040 East, A-119
American Fork, Utah 84003
Kelsaybooks.com

for Brian and Emmet

Acknowledgments

Special thanks to the editors at the following publications where my poems found a home:

Her Words: "9-Months Pregnant at the Presentation," "Work/Life Balance"

Ovunque Siamo (New Italian-American Writing): "Singing Poetry," "A Working Mother's Menu Duplex"

The Paterson Literary Review: "My Son Learns to Speak Flawless French"

Voices in Italian-Americana: "Feminist Sisters"

Special Thanks

To Nathalie Handal, wondrous poet and teacher, who opened my eyes to a world of poets.

To Matthew Lippman, amazing poet, teacher and advisor for your enthusiasm and guidance.

To Maria Mazziotti Gillan, visionary poet, teacher and editor.

To Erv Dea-Jue, good friend and favorite art director partner. You came up with the perfect cover image. Again.

To Fatima Malik, poet and pal, for suggesting I write about advertising.

To Courtney Ryan, sharp, funny daughter-in-law who told me young women would be interested.

To the Italian American Writers Association for fellowship and fun.

To my writing group—Ross Diener, Mary K. O'Melveny and Elen Zanotti—we're small but mighty.

To dear friends who read my poems, come to readings, buy my books: Dorothy, Terry, Alice, John, Miriam, Joe, Ann, Bill, Judith, Neil, Emma & Jo.

And most important, to my husband Brian and my son Emmet who've made this journey a joy.

Contents

PARENTING

WORK 2.0

PARTNERS & OTHER PEOPLE

WORK 1.0

Getting Fired, Laid Off,
Whatever You Want to Call It

At the beginning of my advertising career,
I meet with another Fordham alum
who works at a very creative ad agency.
One of the first things he tells me: “You will be fired.”
It happens all the time.
Not your fault.
The client changes his mind. Staff reductions.
But the thing to remember: “You will find a better job.”

What hopeful and prophetic advice to have gotten
as I repeatedly get fired.
First, for getting married.
Second, for saying “no.”
Third, staff reductions.
After a while, I almost get used to it.

Usually I find a better job:
Senior writer. Supervisor. Creative director.
But it’s stressful.
And all those times, when you’re *not* fired,
they’re upsetting, too.

Some people shun fallen colleagues,
like they’re contagious.
I take them out to lunch.
Tell them to stay in touch.

Next time, it could be me.

The Newest Way to Moisturize Your Skin

Glass half-full
Is the way
I've always looked at life.
Not naïve
Just optimistic.
That made me
a good advertising writer:

"The newest way to moisturize your skin
comes from the pit"
no
"the heart of the apricot."

Shooting Babies

When you're the youngest in a group,
you get the jobs no one else wants.
That's how I end up at photo-shoots
for Johnson's Baby Shampoo.
Trying to get the babies to smile.

It doesn't help that my art director partner
chooses photographers
he'd like to hook up with:
Award-winning nature photographers.
Prima donnas who hide in their offices
until the babies and lights are perfect,
then emerge to snap a few pictures.

Even in those days, I'm trying to
work diversity into casting.
One Hispanic baby to four Nordic ones.
Imagine my delight when the Latin cutie
giggles and glows through his shampoo.

Years later, my own baby loves his bath
and doesn't even notice the shampoo.
It never occurs to me to take a picture.

Hairspray!

By the mid-1970s, most women aren't
buying hairspray.
But my client at Gillette isn't ready to give up.

So we go where women like big hair
and need a little spray
to keep it from drooping.

In Memphis, when I land at midnight
in the middle of the summer,
the radio in the taxi gives the temperature
and humidity both at 99 degrees.
"Am I hearing things?" I ask the driver.
"No, Ma'am. It's that humid."

All those big-haired women in focus groups
confirm our client's hunches.
They still use hairspray.

But I—child of the Sixties—
would never mess up *my* hair
with that stiff, sticky stuff.

Like a Woman

Growing up in the 50s
my parents buy us lots of board games:
Scrabble, Monopoly, Chinese Checkers
and *Careers*.
Careers is my favorite.

Each player comes up with his/her own
success formula—
a combination of love, fame and money.
At a time when marriage and motherhood
are *the* career path for women,
it's refreshing to look at work
like a man.

The careers you can choose are interesting, too:
College brings happiness, perhaps love,
certainly a better salary.
For fame, go to Hollywood.
For money, business school.
Not bad life advice.

By 13, I want be a writer.
Maybe a crusading reporter like *Brenda Starr.* *
I'll have a career plus
marriage and, perhaps, parenthood.

I'll do it somehow.
Like a woman.

* *Brenda Starr first appeared in the* Chicago Tribune Comic Book Magazine *in 1940 and featured a glamorous crusading woman reporter. The strip ran until 2011.*

Lessons We Learn From Our Mothers

In my middle-class family,
Mom and Dad are both college grads.
But Mom doesn't work
after I'm born.
Dad prefers to work two jobs
and have Mom stay at home.
Making delicious meals.
Entertaining their friends.

Don't feel sorry for Dad.
His second job is pure joy—
supervising a recreation center for teens
four nights a week.

How does my mother feel about this?
It's the '50s, so other Moms are at home, too.
Still, I see for myself
our lives revolve around my father.
Dinner no later than 6 pm
so Dad can open the rec center by 7.

Later, when I'm in college,
bemoaning the lack of interesting men,
Mom gives me *the* best advice:
"Concentrate on your career instead."

Birth Name

I'm born a Baldino
but
the O'Hanlon I marry
after college
believes
I deserve a career.

And his parents cheer
my advertising successes.
"That's our girl!"

But the Baldinos—
except for my Mom—
"I love when your commercial comes on!"

All they crave
is the creation
of bambini.

Feminist Sisters

It's a normal morning in the advertising agency where I work.
People greeting each other, getting into the flow of the day.
I'm about to enter my creative director's office.
Phyllis is my mentor, my role model.
A slim, blonde-haired woman in her 40s.
A feminist, she says.
I hesitate briefly at the doorway.
In one of the visitors' chairs sits the eager account executive.
He's saying casually to my boss,
"Wouldn't it be great if Chris dated the client?
I know he likes her. And he's going through a messy divorce."
"What a splendid idea," agrees my heroine.

And I think, "They BOTH want to pimp me out!"
I burst in. "I hate to disappoint you. I'm not dating Ned.
You both know that I'm married."

I slow-walk back to my closet-sized office,
transforming from planet
to my own blazing sun.

The Loneliness of Youth

At first, everyone I work with—
my boss, my art director partners—
is 20 years older than me.
Teachers. Critics. WASPs.

Then a work re-shuffle.
I end up in a group of
New York mixed-nuts.

Only 5 or 10 years older than me,
the other writers are fun.
They like to joke around.
I get an office with a window and door.

At lunchtime, on the day I move in,
there's a party or a brawl —
it's all men's voices, laughing and shouting
next door in Mark's office.
And something keeps hitting our common wall.

Curious, I knock on the closed door.
"Shush! Quiet!" More Laughter. "Do we open the door?"
Mark opens.
"What are you doing in there?" I ask.
"We're playing darts.
And we have a picture of Phyllis as the target."

I'll never know if he's telling the truth.
I'm afraid to look.

Singing Poetry

In the late 1970s, after two job hops,
I land at a very creative ad agency,
a place famous for its musical commercials.
I fit right in. I love writing lyrics.

The one I remember best
is for Nestle Cookie Mix:
"a cookieful of taste."

The line falls out of my mouth.
And my creative director loves it.
We start writing a song about
the three kinds of cookie mixes:

"It's full of sweet, juicy raisins,
It's full of real chocolate morsels,
It's full of chunky peanut butter,
It's a cookieful of taste!"

We cast the commercial in the Fall
But don't shoot until the following Summer.
We hadn't counted on
the 12-year boys' voices changing.

As the director and I watch the rehearsal,
the cute African-American boy
tries to hit the high note: “peanut butter!”

I go to find the creative director.
When I tell him, he smiles.
“Let me hear them,” he says.

We ask the kids to sing again.
The kid’s voice breaks on the high note
and my boss says: “I love it! It’s real!”

GOOD NEWS

9-Months Pregnant at the Presentation

The young men and women in the room are smiling.
But the middle-aged men are bug-eyed
as I stand up to present one of our advertising campaigns.
It's funny, since I know these men are fathers.
They've seen pregnant women.
Just not at a presentation.

I promised the young writer and art directors I supervise
I won't have the baby until after this big meeting.

A ridiculous promise but I don't want them to panic.

While the clients are mesmerized by my belly,
I take advantage.
"Well, if there are no further comments, we'll go forward and
develop these ideas."

Two weeks late, my son waits
to make his own beautiful
8 lb. 7 oz. presentation.

Becoming a Mother.
And Everything Is New.

Nothing prepared me for you.
The love I feel instantly.
The way your dark blue eyes never leave my face.
Like you are memorizing it.
The way everything is new for you.
New for me, too.
The way I miss you when I leave the house.
and go for a 15-minute walk.
The way I hear your tiniest cry
and get up to nurse you.
Your first smile. Your first giggle.
You are our very best creation.

“And suddenly, I’m mentally defective.”

When I return to work three months after giving birth,
my creative director begins to treat me differently.

He’s the same man who called me at home
when the doctors thought I might have phlebitis,
and asked me if I could write a new radio campaign.

The same man who panicked when I took a two-week vacation
for a family trip to Ireland.

The father of three children who never asks about my baby.

All that I would have excused, but not the way he won’t
look me in the eye. Give me assignments. Include me in planning.

I’m sent on a focus group trip to who-knows-where
and get to talking to the couple who run the groups.
They suggest I talk to another creative director at my agency
who’s a new mother, too. Overworked. And exhausted.

That’s how I start working with wonderful Susan.

The Shrink Deals with Feminist Disillusionment at the First Visit

"What kind of work do you do?"
is her first question.
And from my mouth,
for the next 40 minutes
falls a tale of betrayals
at the hands of other women.

My first boss, Eve, who fires me.
For getting married.

The creative director, Phyllis,
who rescues me
from typing scripts
to write tie-dye ads to teenagers.
I'd do anything for her.
Record radio testimonials? Yes.
Travel for business? Of course.
Service the client? Hell, no!

It's five years since Phyllis.
I have a woman boss again.
Susan seems great.
A new mother like me.
Gives me lots of responsibility.
I'm afraid to trust her 100%.

The shrink explains:
"No need to trust anyone 100%."

Mother-to-Mother Shorthand

Working with Susan is like a dream.

One minute, she's confiding the difficulty
of having two children under 3-years old—
she had hurried to have a second son.

The next I'm telling her the details about my trip
the following week to Orlando,
to photograph *Avon ladies* with their mothers,
a Mothers' Day promotion.

I remember coming down with bronchitis
(I'd probably caught it from Emmet, my 18-month-old son)
the same week I'm recording a new radio show,
Feeling Beautiful for Avon.
I'm taking antibiotics but still coughing a lot.

"Is it okay if I just go to the recording studio
and not come into the office?"
"Of course. Feel better."

Why couldn't all creative directors work like this?

The Devil Wears Prada

Viewing *The Devil Wears Prada* the second time,
I'm struck by how much my first creative director, Phyllis,
resembles the Meryl Streep character.
The WASP snobbism. The arrogance.
And I'm reminded of all the stuff I had to brush off
for *the honor* of that job.

All the times Phyllis reminds me how grateful
I should feel. The careless remarks
about my Italian-American background,
my Fordham education.

7 years and 2 agencies later, I'm doing
the best work of my career.
Phyllis tracks me down.
Asks me to meet her latest mentee.
Here's what I tell the young woman:
"Don't be afraid to move on."

Disguising a Hippie

Luna is a lovely kid from LA.
Her folks run a bookshop on the Sunset Strip.
She has multiple nose and ear piercings.
It doesn't faze me.
Her work is stellar.

I want to bring her to an Avon client meeting
but the client is so suburban.
I'm afraid Luna's appearance
might jeopardize the acceptance of her work.

"Luna," I explain, "I'd like to bring you
to meet the client. But he's a real square.
Could you lose the nose rings for the meeting?"

"Sure," she says. "Anything else?"
"Well, now that mention it, do you have another coat
in place of the red shaggy one?"
"Yes, I do."

The Avon client loves Luna's work.
When we get back to the Agency,
Luna tells her teammates.
Meanwhile, I drop by to tell Susan.
She's pleased. Then she leans
across her desk, and says quietly,
"So, Luna has another coat? Nice work."

The Culture of a Company

I don't notice until I'm in my thirties
how the character of an ad agency's creative director
shapes everyone in the department—
writers, art directors, TV producers.

If the person is ethical and generous,
he/she hires similar people.
And vice versa.
When the creative director who hired Susan
decides to retire, he passes the baton
to his most successful group creative director.

Paul didn't really want the job—
but he takes it anyway.
The pressure makes his drinking worse.
The affair with his secretary becomes open.
He hires old friends—hacks and crooks—for big jobs.
That sets the tone:
Everyone is free to drink, do drugs, and sleep around.

Right after the change, Susan attends a weekend away
for upper management. Spouses are not invited.
The scene on Saturday night, after dinner, is horrifying—
men she works with chasing her back to her hotel room.
Drunk or high on coke, they assume she'll let them in.

After that, Susan is determined to leave.
Soon she's offered freelance work from an old client.

Meanwhile I'm transferred to another group.
I write award-winning ads for Lucite paint.
But the creative director is hitting on me. Openly.
Entertainment for his side-kicks.

I tell my husband, "Soon I'll be fired."

Unemployed in my thirties, I ask myself, "What's so great about advertising?"

Okay   you've just spent the last 10 years
doing what you love   doing it well   by objective standards
sales   awards   TV on the agency's new business reel.

And you're fired.

Because you wouldn't   fill in the blanks.
Is the Universe trying to tell you something?
Please be clearer, Universe.

I could still write snappy headlines   Come up with concepts
It was easy to freelance.
No questions.   No commitments.

My son is in his last year   of posh nursery school.
The other parents know   I'm not working full-time.

"Did you do something wrong, Mommy?" asks 5-year-old Emmet.
"No, sweetie. Just bad luck."

PARENTING

Being One of Two Working Mothers at the Posh Nursery School

The school has no language for me.
Or for the other mother, a lawyer.
The teachers will not understand
our need to get to work.

The other mothers regard us
as another species. Suspect.
They huddle in groups,
like middle school,
coiffed and smartly dressed
for coffee with one another.

When they want something,
these women are like mafia:
"Your son *has* to come for a playdate.
I'll send the driver to pick him up.
What do you mean *no*?"

My husband experiences this strangeness, too.
Only he and another father show up
for school plays or book sales.
If he offers his help, he notes,
"The women don't know what to do with me."

When it's time to move on,
we choose the United Nations School.
The headmistress is disappointed.
She wants our bright son to go to Dalton.

"People like us go to Dalton or Collegiate."

"Us?"
Hadn't she noticed
we aren't alike at all.

Easter Bunny

Do kids know when we have to
get to work on time,
or get to a doctor's appointment,
and deliberately slow us down?

Or are they all just dawdlers,
especially in the morning?

I still remember a morning in April.
My son, Emmet, is 4.
And he's stalling.
Talking about the Easter Bunny.
Impatient, I say, "Oh, Emmet,
you know there's no Easter Bunny."

"What?" He's crestfallen.
"I mean, there's no Easter Bunny in Manhattan.
He lives on a vegetable farm on Long Island."

Mother's Helpers in the 1980s

Not my parents, generous and volatile,
who act like noisy two-year-olds.

Not our neighbor, an editor at Reader's Digest,
who means well but is an alcoholic.

Not my sharp, funny mother-in-law,
newly retired, lover of books,
who travels an hour on express bus
to take care of her grandson.
She's my childcare encyclopedia.

No, the mother's helpers are two students
I hire from NYU, friends and art majors.
They pick up our son from nursery school
three days a week.

Donna, hands-on artistic—I come home from work
to find *Play-doh* villages or finger-paint masterpieces
on the dining room table.

Marina, musical—she plays
our precious Beatles LPs on
our son's Fisher-Price record player.
I open the apartment door to hear
both of them singing
Lucy in the Sky with Diamonds
at the top of their lungs.

Booklovers

for Emmet

We start with sturdy cardboard,
Pat The Bunny and
graduate to picture books,
Richard Scarry's
What Do People Do All Day?

Before long, we're walking to Donnell Library
or taking the M4 bus to *Eeyore's,* that wonderful
children's book store that loses its lease.
While I try to steer you to fiction,
you always head to history—
the Revolutionary War, the Underground Railroad.
I let you choose 4 or 5 titles, then slip in one for me:
Willy Wonka and the Chocolate Factory.

I remember taking turns reading
chapters of *Huck Finn*
when you were 8 or 9,
discussing friendship and freedom,
and the breaking of bad laws.

Then, when you're 10,
you announce
you can read by yourself.

I have to wait
until your daughter is 6-months old
to share *Pat the Bunny*
with a new budding book-lover.

A Working Mother's Menu Duplex

We have easy dinners during the week.
We please ourselves with good simple food.

    Pasta and salads are good simple food.
    A nutritionist might not approve.

Grandma, a nutritionist, might not approve.
We love Grandma but we don't tell her.

    There are other things we don't tell her.
    We don't mention you run track *and* play soccer.

She'd worry you'd get injured playing soccer.
But you're athletic and don't get hurt.

    You're a good student and sports don't hurt.
    Dad works nights as a news editor.

Weekends arrive even for news editors.
Dad and I cook up a storm every weekend.

My Son Learns French at the UN School

"Mommy," says 6-year-old Emmet,
"French is such a funny language.
You have to use your nose for some sounds.
And roll your tongue."
"Wow!" I say. I learned French in high school.
My accent is atrocious.

His teachers begin with games and songs.
They make it fun.
A concept my French teachers had never heard of.
And the only downside, from my point of view,
is the constant question my husband and I get at
parent-teacher conferences: "Do you speak French at home?"
To which we have to answer: "Non."

At the beginning of third grade,
I get a call at work.
"Bonjour, this is Madame Rochet. I'm the director
of the French department at UNIS.
Do you speak French at home?"
"No, Madame," I explain our deficiencies.
"Well, Emmet loves French.
Would it be all right if we put him in a class
with Francophones?"
"Yes, I'm sure he'd love it."

Four years later, we find ourselves
at the Musée de la Ville de Paris.
A group of Americans in the gift store
are shouting at a salesperson.

"Emmet," I ask, "*C*an you go over there
and sort things out?"
My young diplomat just nods
and walks over.

The Parents' Fundraiser for the UN School

It's always on a Saturday in the Spring.
Parents make food from their home countries
and serve it for lunch:
Spanish tortilla de patatas, Turkish kabobs, Indian samosas.
The flavors and aromas are wonderful.
I bake loaves of Irish brown bread which
a parent from the Irish consulate
reserves in advance.

After lunch, there are boisterous carnival games in the gym,
manned by the parents.
One year, I handle the game with plastic bowling pins.
The kids knock them over. I reset them.
When my hour is up, I have a splitting headache.

My mother-in-law has come along.
We take a taxi home.
"Dorothy," I admit, "My head is throbbing."
"Yes," she says kindly. "My friend Lucia and I
always took two aspirins before going to these things.
The noise alone is enough to kill you."

And I think, she sent her three sons to Catholic school
in the Bronx.
We're sending Emmet to the United Nations School
in Manhattan.

It doesn't matter where you take your pain-killers.

Watching My Son Play Soccer in Riverdale

I've just dropped Emmet and his friend Ganesh off with their coach. We had to taxi here—to this cars-only private school in Riverdale's hills.

Now I'm sitting alone in the stands. A luxury in my work/family-filled life.

Normally I come with my husband but he's leading a journalists' trip to China. Four months of planning and chopsticks practice.

It's the first time I've met my son's soccer coach. He gave me a warm smile. Yikes. When did coaches get so young and handsome?

My son attends *Hunter College High School*, an elite public school in Manhattan. The game is at *Horace Mann*, a private prep school in the north of the borough.

From up here in the bleachers, I have a great view of the field. The Fall foliage is stunning—reds, golds, oranges, show off in the sun.

I'm surrounded by *Horace Mann* parents. They stepped out of a *J.Crew* catalog. Now I've spotted some *Hunter* parents on the field in their Saturday clothes—old jackets, raincoats, scarves.

And suddenly I'm scrambling down the bleachers to join them.

I want to shout, "Go Emmet! Go Ganesh!" into this glorious October day.

WORK 2.0

A Good Friend Throws Me a Lifeline

My friend and former partner, Shelley K.,
tells me about direct advertising.
It's TV and print ads that
include a phone number.

She sets up an interview for me
with a group creative director at Ogilvy.
While I wait in reception, I'm blown away
by the creativity of the work on the walls.

I don't get the job—but I get curious.
NYU has an evening class from 7 to 9.
My Mom comes to the rescue.
She and Dad come down from the Bronx to babysit.

Buoyed by an enthusiastic teacher,
I begin creating new work for my portfolio.
I imagine three different clubs for
the Museum of Natural History—
for families, for singles, for seniors.
And three direct advertising campaigns.

I also come up with a light-hearted campaign
to lure vacationers back to Bermuda.
I put a little bag of pink sand
(I saved from our honeymoon)
into a letter urging travelers to return.

This kind of thinking gets me a new interview at Ogilvy.
And this time, after some awkward questions,
I get the job.

Those Interview Questions

"Why do you want to leave general advertising?"
asks John, my potential creative director.
And I'm not ready,
as nice as John seems,
to talk about the sexism,
the drugs, the drinking.
It's 1985, decades away from *MeToo.*
So instead, I talk about the hacks and
formulaic ads some agencies are famous for.
John knows there's something I'm not saying.
but he lets it go.

Then I meet Tina,
the group creative director,
John's boss.
Toward the end of our 30-minute chat,
Tina asks, so casually,

"Do you think you'll be happy
working in direct advertising?"

"I wouldn't be happy at a lot
of direct agencies," I admit,
"But I think I'll be happy at Ogilvy."

"I think so, too,"
agrees Tina.

The Culture of Ogilvy Direct

It begins with the smiling doorman saying, “Good morning.”
Soon he’ll know your name, and you’ll know his.
People milling at the elevators look happy.
They make eye contact. They greet each other.

Inside, the building is a warren of little offices—
An old carpet factory, I hear.
This was Park Avenue South, a neighborhood of
Turkish carpet sellers and furniture showrooms.

I have four art director partners, all talented.
They appreciate that I “brainstorm” ideas with them,
a practice I take from general advertising.

My group creative director is Tina.
Her son, Will, is a few years younger than Emmet.
Tina asks me to recommend a summer day camp.
Soon Will is going there, too.

I know Tina defends me on at least one occasion,
when a male supervisor says he loves everything about me,
except that I have to leave at 5:30 to pick up my son.

Tina’s rejoinder: “Chris wouldn’t be the same writer
if she wasn’t a mother.”

Pitching Baggage Insurance Is Just the Beginning

One of my first jobs at Ogilvy is a new business pitch
to get American Express Baggage Insurance.
I take my own experience—traveling so much
on business in my twenties.

I begin a letter with this headline:

"I stood watching the empty baggage carousel
go round and round, wondering . . .
where had my bag gone?"

American Express does a mail test. My letter gets a 5% response.
"That's crazy good," I learn.
We get the account.

Other products are not so easy.
Credit card registry. A great service if your wallet is lost or stolen.
But no one (except in New York City) expects that to happen.

Flight insurance. Other financial products.
This was a far cry from cookie mixes.
I realize my job is to make complicated stuff
easy to understand.
First, I have to digest it. I do this at night
in that brief hour between Emmet going to sleep
and my husband coming home from work.

I begin getting by on six hours of sleep.

Searching for Sisterhood

Maybe it's like love.
No point looking.
Just let it come.

I spend my twenties
in advertising.
It's not there.

I lose my job.
Two years later I find myself
in direct marketing.

Tina, my group creative director,
is defending me to male bosses
Re: my motherhood.

I'm not making it up.
Maybe a meritocracy like DM
works better for women.

You need to know your craft.
No faking your way
writing an interactive mailing,

A website, an e-zine,
A poster campaign.
In advertising, it's easier to pose:

Write a good headline.
Do a sketch or two.
Let someone else execute it.

Just saying.
I was blinded by the star power
of TV commercials,

big budgets, big agencies.
But I'm happier
being part of the galaxy.

Innocent Adventurer

No matter where I work,
Mom takes the Express Bus from the Bronx—
to meet me for lunch.
She's undaunted by un-Disneyfied Times Square.
She enjoys stylish *B. Smith's* as much as vegan Chinese.
At heart, she's a good food enthusiast.

And I think she needs a break from Dad.
He has to retire at 64—he's become blind in one eye.
Mom is coping with having him home 24/7.
She needs to assert her independence. If only for lunch.

The Shrink Solves a Work Situation

Dr. R. has a comfortable office on the Upper East Side
where I see her before work,
about once a month.
Today my problem: My boss is going to work in London
for 3–6 months.
I worry how I will I do his job *and* mine at the same time.

"No, you can't do two jobs," Dr. R. says matter-of-factly.
"You'll do his job. And hire someone to do yours."
"That's brilliant," I say, greatly relieved.
She laughs, a wonderful, silvery sound.

Jazzing Up Agency Day

Our American Express Air Flight Insurance clients
feel less important than their colleagues
who market the Amex Card.

To boost their self-esteem,
I work with our film department
to create a 10-minute compilation of funny scenes
from airline disaster movies: *Airplane,*
Those Magnificent Men in their Flying Machines, etc.
to show them on Agency Day.

The clients roar with delight
when they see the short film.
I give them a copy to bring back to Amex.

No more flying the cheap seats.

PARTNERS & OTHER PEOPLE

"Who says only bad guys get their picture in the Post Office?"

Over the course of a career
you get a hunch,
call it intuition,
that an art director will be a great partner.
It might be his wacky sense of humor.
His cool sense of design.
Whatever—I get that with Erv.
A feeling that 1+1 will make 3.

Erv has a way of finding gold
in my off-the-wall observations.
Take the new US Postal Stamps for American Folk Heroes—
Paul Bunyan, John Henry and Johnny Appleseed.

The headline becomes:
"Who says only bad guys
get their pictures in the Post Office?"

I do the same for him.
"Presidents. Statesmen. Rabbits."
is his funny, strange, attention-getting headline.

But no stranger than the assignment:
re-introducing the *George Washington* and *Ben Franklin* stamps
at the same time as introducing *Bugs Bunny*.

If Your Passion Is Coffee

Such an advertising story:

Getting a phone call
8 pm on a Friday night
while entertaining friends.

The Creative Director:
“The Agency is pitching Gervalia coffee.
Could you come in Sunday to help?”

Ordinarily I could.
But Sunday was Mother’s Day.
I had invited my Mom and Mother-in-law
for lunch.

Counter offer:
“Could I work Saturday
writing headlines
and email them to her?”

“That would be fine.”

So I spend Saturday
drinking Gervalia
thinking about European cafes—
the freshly-brewed coffee, the aroma,
the smooth, delicious taste.

This headline emerges from my over-caffeinated brain:
"If your passion is coffee,
your pleasure will be Gervalia."

Something Is Rotten at the Agency

Tina is recruited as Chief Creative Officer
and President for a large Direct Agency.
A year later, I join her there.

Her success winning big accounts—
AT&T, Citibank, US Postal Stamps, Gervalia—
is amazing.

But now, six years later, there are rumors of change.
The general agency is poaching Direct's clients.
Other clients are leaving.

I sense, rather than know, Tina is moving on.

At the same time, I can't seem to talk to her.
It's like a wall has come down between us.
I don't learn about her illness for another 5 years.

Musical Intervals

In times of unemployment,
my cousin Joyce makes it her mission
to lift my spirits.

She hops the train from Hastings-on-Hudson
and takes me to jazz concerts at lunch:
the sexy voice of Dee Dee Bridgewater.
Bucky Pizzarelli's magical guitar.

Or we go to museum and gallery shows.
We discover Klimt, Matisse's cut-outs,
Bonnard's palette of joyous colors.

Joyce always says, "It's hard to feel sad
when you're listening to Bucky or
being transported
by a buoyant Bonnard."

Working Mothers

Another move. Another agency.

Another former Ogilvy colleague
is the Creative Director.

Shelley is brilliant. She inspires loyalty and affection.

We talk clients in meetings.
But elevator conversations are all about our sons.

Like half the agency—over 100 people—I work on Bank of America.
creating out-of-home advertising, posters for big places—
Yankee Stadium, Shea Stadium, Fenway Park.

I also do ads for *inside* the bank—selling checking accounts, CDs,
lines of credit. I become the queen of fine print.

Then, out of the blue, Bank of America pulls its business.
It doesn't make sense—their sales are terrific.
But by then I realize these decisions are made
at men's clubs. And on golf courses.

On top of this, Shelley's cancer returns.
This time with a vengeance.

This Layoff Is Particularly Brutal

What sadist designed this plan
to break up friends,
partners and creative groups?
To send people to 3 different meeting rooms
to learn their fates?

I'm not safe *exactly.*
I'm not fired either.
I'm in limbo—
being sent to a small sister agency
I've never heard of.
For how long?
To work on what?

This has happened so many times.
But today, I have a pain in my chest.
I go home. My husband is there.
He gives me a bear hug and a diazepam.
Tells me to take a nap.

I awaken two hours later, and I'm fine.
I can get through this.
I've been through much worse.
Times I lost a job and my husband was freelancing.
Times we worried about college tuition.

"You were working without a net,"
my grown son observes years later.
I laugh in rccognition,
and think, "What a perceptive kid."

The Cost of Success in a Man's World

I succeed in my own way
as a group creative director.

I'm never *the* creative director of an Agency.
Well, only at a small place.
And only for a year.
I hate the job.
No one to talk to.
No one to trust.
Plus, competing agendas of the main partners.

When I think of women, like Tina and Shelley,
Chief Creative Officers of big, successful ad agencies,
so smart and talented, yet no match
for the machinations of men.

Shelley's husband believes the snarky work situation
helped kill his wife with stress.
Even though it was cancer, officially.

And I wonder if Tina's early-onset illness
is stress-related.

It’s funny that men in big jobs can go
from failure to failure,
getting endless do-overs.

Not women.
We get one shot.
And it better be a three-point basket.

Serendipity

I hear through the grapevine
that Grey Advertising in pitching Citibank,
an account I've worked on.

I also hear that the Creative Director
is fun to work for.

I phone her directly for a job in financial services.
She looks at my portfolio of work and says,
"You have an empathetic voice. You'd be perfect for healthcare."

I'll spend the next ten years—not selling people drugs—
but persuading them to take their Rx correctly.
offering lifestyle tips to help them feel better.
It's called *compliance*—the kind of thing doctors
don't have time to do.

I'll help people with migraines, allergies, sinus problems,
arthritis, Crohn's disease, macular degeneration.

I’ll write websites, encouraging emails, friendly letters.
I’ll create web magazines.

I have colleagues who become hypochondriacs
doing this work.

I become immensely grateful.

In the Flow

When I work as a freelance advertising writer,
I have no office.
Only a desk, a computer, sometimes a low wall
Dividing my space from others
Writers and art directors
In a conference room.

To hear myself think
I wear noise-cancelling headphones
And I listen to the music
Of the rain.
It's my eye
In the storm of distractions
And conversations.
It's my calm.
From there I can wander
And wonder
"What do I want to say?
How do I want to say it?"

It doesn't matter what I'm writing
An email campaign
A web-magazine
A poster

My mind and fingers
On the computer keys
Can create the pathways.
I disappear
Into the flow.

Occasionally, someone interrupts
With a question, a comment,
A tap on the shoulder.
I remove the headphones
Forgetting to turn down the volume.
And everyone around me
Turns around and shouts,
“Turn down that noise!”
I grin, unplug the headphones,
And say with surprise,
“Oh, really, you don’t like the rain?”

How to Freelance Forever

After a certain age, it's hard for men and women
to get a staff job.
But freelance work is always available
if you know your craft.

You can't bluff your way through writing website copy,
E-zines, or interactive email.
You have to be able to write a good headline, sure,
but also paragraphs of copy.

It can be liberating to become a freelancer in your fifties.
Especially if you land a gig that lasts a year or two.
The pay is great. There's very little politics.
Just make sure you have health insurance.

LATER

If I Had Known

Would I have chosen advertising
for a career?

If someone had mentioned *male bastion*
or *misogyny?*
Perhaps an instructor at Fordham?
Or an alum?

Was it the times?
Anti-War. Civil Rights.
Betty Friedan. Gloria Steinem.
Was the desire for change in the air?

Was I optimistic?
Over-confident?
Over-committed?
Yes, all of the above.

Would I do it again?

For the pleasure of crafting a great headline?
For the fun of working with a smart art director partner?
For the smiles I witnessed from my singing commercial?

Yes, I probably would.

Despite the deadly deadlines.
Impossible bosses.
Dull clients.

The relentless layoffs.

Yes, I'd do it again.

In a heartbeat.

A conversation with the soul of Tina as though we still had offices next door to each other at Ogilvy

How I wish that cruel illness   hadn't crushed you.
You were brilliant.   A great creative director.

For too long   I thought you were angry at me.
Then   too late   I realized you were gone.

You taught me so much   about managing people
winning Echo and Andy awards   exploring new mediums.
You understood   that my being a mother
was part   of the writer I am.

I wish you were here   so we could talk about our boys.
Will and Emmet.   Emmet's a bad-ass US attorney.

I know you'd love that.   And I have a
granddaughter.
Finally, a girl.

Still, I'm certain we'll meet   in that creative section of heaven
where the cool spirits hang out   making music and poetry.

Though I'm pretty sure   they won't need advertising.

Your Work in the World

If you're lucky   and loved   and told you deserve a career

one will appear   first as an apparition   almost a dream

except you've prepared for it   all your life

doing what you love   what you do well.

I loved writing   making films   it made sense

to write TV commercials   for   Nestle Cookie Mix.

Naturally, you'll need to be driven   since you're a woman.

Be prepared to be bored   stressed   and   exhausted.

And then   because change   is the thing you can count on

your career at   20   30   60   70   will   evolve.

You can have it all   work, love, leisure   but not

at the same time.

Work/Life Balance

You ask me how I did it, work full-time
as a senior writer, a creative director,
and still make time to be a good mother.
You have your own children now,
and work you love, "most of the time."
"Most of the time," being the best
anyone can hope for.

So, I tell you about the Saturday morning
you helped me with work.
You were 7-years old and loved to rhyme.
Together we wrote an invitation
for a holiday party, to the tune of
Deck the Halls with Boughs of Holly. I think.
It was thirty years ago.

I'm not sure how helpful this is for you.
You're a prosecutor. Putting armed robbers,
sex offenders, fentanyl peddlers in jail.
But it leads to a discussion of other jobs
you've been offered. Less work. More money.
But unfortunately, boring. At least for you.
You know adrenaline is your drug of choice.
You've known that since college when
you became a volunteer EMT.

I asked you then if you wanted to be a doctor.
You said, no, you just loved “the rush.”
Dad and I got that. Dad with his news deadlines.
Me with new business presentations.

So, I circle back and remind you that right now—
two kids under 6—is the most labor-intensive.
It will get easier. You already see it with your daughter.
Bright and funny, learning to read. A good sleeper.

And now we’re back in the driveway—
we made a pizza run—and you still want to talk.
You’re yawning. “This has been a hell of a week.
Getting to bed at midnight. Getting up at 6.
Next week will be better.”

About the Author

Christine's first career was writing advertising—TV, print, online—for credit cards and cookie mixes. She retired from advertising when her first grandchild was born, and was inspired to return to writing poetry.

The Bronx Years, her first collection (Finishing Line Press, 2023), recalls her rebellion growing up in an Italian-American family in the Bronx, NY. In *SEARCHING for SISTERHOOD,* her poems take you inside the male bastion of advertising in the 1970s, working motherhood in the '80s, finding sisterly support in unexpected places.

Her poems appear in *Her Words, Paterson Literary Review, Voices in Italian-Americana*, *Ovunque Siamo* (New Italian-American Writing), *Jerry Jazz Musician, Silver Birch Press,* and in the anthology *Rumors, Secrets & Lies.* Christine lives with her husband Brian on the Upper Eastside of Manhattan.

www.ingramcontent.com/pod-product-compliance
Lightning Source LLC
LaVergne TN
LVHW051016080826
845145LV00009B/2652

9781639808502